The first stories in the Bible talk about God as creator. They tell about God making the world and everything in it. There is a song in the Bible called **Psalm 8** in which the author talks about some of the things God has made. It's as if the person who wrote the psalm looked at many things in the world and said, "Wow! God, the world is filled with awesome things!"

Do you ever wonder, "Who is God?"

What are things in the world that make you say "Wow!"?
Write a prayer or blessing about these things.

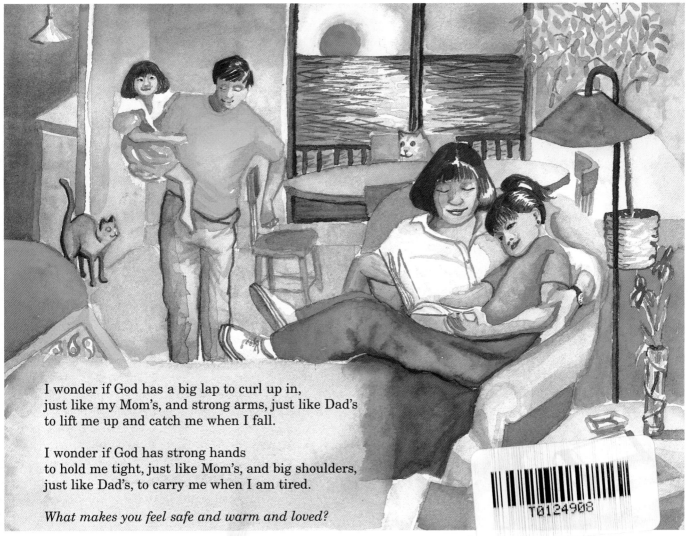

I wonder if God has a big lap to curl up in,
just like my Mom's, and strong arms, just like Dad's
to lift me up and catch me when I fall.

I wonder if God has strong hands
to hold me tight, just like Mom's, and big shoulders,
just like Dad's, to carry me when I am tired.

What makes you feel safe and warm and loved?

Do you ever ask yourself, "What is God like?"
Lots of people do that.
People think of God in lots of different
ways: as father, mother, creator, friend.
How do you like to think of God?
What do you think God might look like?
What things make you think about God:
what colors, feelings, smells, sounds?

Can you draw a picture of God? It's difficul[
Draw a picture of what God might be like
a picture of something God does. Or, draw
picture of a time when you felt God's presence
when you felt the nearness of God.

God is like _____

_____

God does _____

_____

I feel the nearness of God when _____

_____

Sometimes I think God is just like my Dad
when he holds the back seat of my new two wheel bicycle
just long enough for me to catch my balance.
Then he lets go, and I ride all by myself!
But it's nice to know he's running right alongside me.

The first stories in the Bible talk about God as creator. They tell about God making the world and everything in it. There is a song in the Bible called **Psalm 8** in which the author talks about some of the things God has made.

It's as if the person who wrote the psalm looked at many things in the world and said, "Wow! God, the world is filled with awesome things!"

Do you ever wonder, "Who is God?"

What are things in the world that make you say "Wow!"?
Write a prayer or blessing about these things.

I wonder if God has a big lap to curl up in,
just like my Mom's, and strong arms, just like Dad's
to lift me up and catch me when I fall.

I wonder if God has strong hands
to hold me tight, just like Mom's, and big shoulders,
just like Dad's, to carry me when I am tired.

What makes you feel safe and warm and loved?

Do you ever ask yourself, "What is God like?"
Lots of people do that.
People think of God in lots of different
ways: as father, mother, creator, friend.
How do you like to think of God?
What do you think God might look like?
What things make you think about God:
what colors, feelings, smells, sounds?

Can you draw a picture of God? It's difficult
Draw a picture of what God might be like o
a picture of something God does. Or, draw a
picture of a time when you felt God's presence o
when you felt the nearness of God.

God is like _____

_____

God does _____

_____

I feel the nearness of God when _____

_____

Sometimes I think God is just like my Dad
when he holds the back seat of my new two wheel bicycle
just long enough for me to catch my balance.
Then he lets go, and I ride all by myself!
But it's nice to know he's running right alongside me.

The first stories in the Bible talk about God as creator. They tell about God making the world and everything in it. There is a song in the Bible called **Psalm 8** in which the author talks about some of the things God has made.

It's as if the person who wrote the psalm looked at many things in the world and said, "Wow! God, the world is filled with awesome things!"

Do you ever wonder, "Who is God?"

**What are things in the world that make you say "Wow!"?
Write a prayer or blessing about these things.**

I wonder if God has a big lap to curl up in,
just like my Mom's, and strong arms, just like Dad's
to lift me up and catch me when I fall.

I wonder if God has strong hands
to hold me tight, just like Mom's, and big shoulders,
just like Dad's, to carry me when I am tired.

What makes you feel safe and warm and loved?

Do you ever ask yourself, "What is God like?"
Lots of people do that.
People think of God in lots of different
ways: as father, mother, creator, friend.
How do you like to think of God?
What do you think God might look like?
What things make you think about God:
what colors, feelings, smells, sounds?

Can you draw a picture of God? It's difficult
Draw a picture of what God might be like o
a picture of something God does. Or, draw
picture of a time when you felt God's presence o
when you felt the nearness of God.

God is like _____

_____

God does _____

_____

I feel the nearness of God when _____

_____

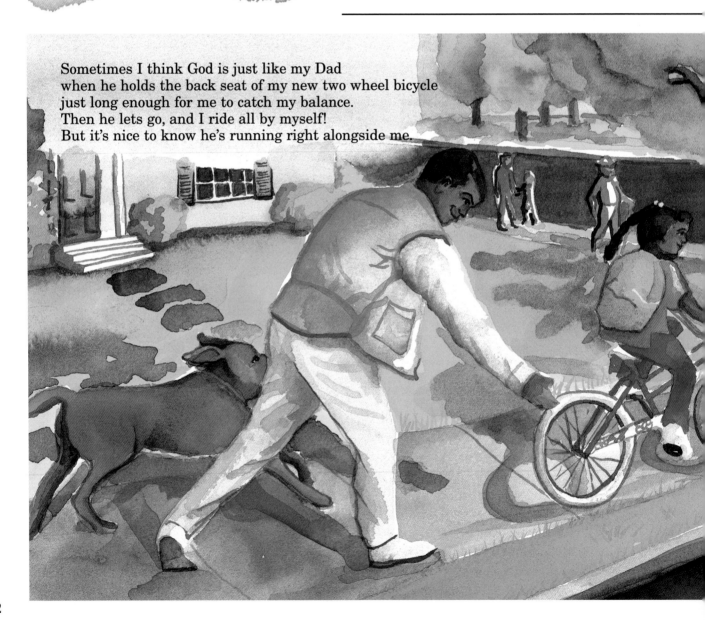

Sometimes I think God is just like my Dad
when he holds the back seat of my new two wheel bicycle
just long enough for me to catch my balance.
Then he lets go, and I ride all by myself!
But it's nice to know he's running right alongside me.

What Is God Like?

The first stories in the Bible talk about God as creator. They tell about God making the world and everything in it. There is a song in the Bible called **Psalm 8** in which the author talks about some of the things God has made.

It's as if the person who wrote the psalm looked at many things in the world and said, "Wow! God, the world is filled with awesome things!"

Do you ever wonder, "Who is God?"

**What are things in the world that make you say "Wow!"?
Write a prayer or blessing about these things.**

I wonder if God has a big lap to curl up in,
just like my Mom's, and strong arms, just like Dad's
to lift me up and catch me when I fall.

I wonder if God has strong hands
to hold me tight, just like Mom's, and big shoulders,
just like Dad's, to carry me when I am tired.

What makes you feel safe and warm and loved?

Do you ever ask yourself, "What is God like?"
Lots of people do that.
People think of God in lots of different
ways: as father, mother, creator, friend.
How do you like to think of God?
What do you think God might look like?
What things make you think about God:
what colors, feelings, smells, sounds?

Can you draw a picture of God? It's difficult!
Draw a picture of what God might be like or
a picture of something God does. Or, draw a
picture of a time when you felt God's presence or
when you felt the nearness of God.

God is like _____

_____

God does _____

_____

I feel the nearness of God when _____

_____

Sometimes I think God is just like my Dad
when he holds the back seat of my new two wheel bicycle
just long enough for me to catch my balance.
Then he lets go, and I ride all by myself!
But it's nice to know he's running right alongside me.

What Is God Like?

The first stories in the Bible talk about God as creator. They tell about God making the world and everything in it. There is a song in the Bible called **Psalm 8** in which the author talks about some of the things God has made. It's as if the person who wrote the psalm looked at many things in the world and said, "Wow! God, the world is filled with awesome things!"

Do you ever wonder, "Who is God?"

What are things in the world that make you say "Wow!"? Write a prayer or blessing about these things.

I wonder if God has a big lap to curl up in,
just like my Mom's, and strong arms, just like Dad's
to lift me up and catch me when I fall.

I wonder if God has strong hands
to hold me tight, just like Mom's, and big shoulders,
just like Dad's, to carry me when I am tired.

What makes you feel safe and warm and loved?

Do you ever ask yourself, "What is God like?"
Lots of people do that.
People think of God in lots of different ways: as father, mother, creator, friend.
How do you like to think of God?
What do you think God might look like?
What things make you think about God: what colors, feelings, smells, sounds?

Can you draw a picture of God? It's difficult
Draw a picture of what God might be like o
a picture of something God does. Or, draw
picture of a time when you felt God's presence o
when you felt the nearness of God.

God is like _____

_____

God does _____

_____

I feel the nearness of God when _____

_____

Sometimes I think God is just like my Dad
when he holds the back seat of my new two wheel bicycle
just long enough for me to catch my balance.
Then he lets go, and I ride all by myself!
But it's nice to know he's running right alongside me.

The first stories in the Bible talk about God as creator. They tell about God making the world and everything in it. There is a song in the Bible called **Psalm 8** in which the author talks about some of the things God has made. It's as if the person who wrote the psalm looked at many things in the world and said, "Wow! God, the world is filled with awesome things!"

Do you ever wonder, "Who is God?"

**What are things in the world that make you say "Wow!"?
Write a prayer or blessing about these things.**

I wonder if God has a big lap to curl up in,
just like my Mom's, and strong arms, just like Dad's
to lift me up and catch me when I fall.

I wonder if God has strong hands
to hold me tight, just like Mom's, and big shoulders,
just like Dad's, to carry me when I am tired.

What makes you feel safe and warm and loved?

Do you ever ask yourself, "What is God like?"
Lots of people do that.
People think of God in lots of different ways: as father, mother, creator, friend.
How do you like to think of God?
What do you think God might look like?
What things make you think about God: what colors, feelings, smells, sounds?

Can you draw a picture of God? It's difficult! Draw a picture of what God might be like or a picture of something God does. Or, draw a picture of a time when you felt God's presence or when you felt the nearness of God.

God is like _____

_____

God does _____

_____

I feel the nearness of God when _____

_____

Sometimes I think God is just like my Dad
when he holds the back seat of my new two wheel bicycle
just long enough for me to catch my balance.
Then he lets go, and I ride all by myself!
But it's nice to know he's running right alongside me.

What Is God Like?

The first stories in the Bible talk about God as creator. They tell about God making the world and everything in it. There is a song in the Bible called **Psalm 8** in which the author talks about some of the things God has made.

It's as if the person who wrote the psalm looked at many things in the world and said, "Wow! God, the world is filled with awesome things!"

Do you ever wonder, "Who is God?"

**What are things in the world that make you say "Wow!"?
Write a prayer or blessing about these things.**

I wonder if God has a big lap to curl up in,
just like my Mom's, and strong arms, just like Dad's
to lift me up and catch me when I fall.

I wonder if God has strong hands
to hold me tight, just like Mom's, and big shoulders,
just like Dad's, to carry me when I am tired.

What makes you feel safe and warm and loved?

Do you ever ask yourself, "What is God like?"
Lots of people do that.
People think of God in lots of different ways: as father, mother, creator, friend.
How do you like to think of God?
What do you think God might look like?
What things make you think about God: what colors, feelings, smells, sounds?

Can you draw a picture of God? It's difficult. Draw a picture of what God might be like or a picture of something God does. Or, draw a picture of a time when you felt God's presence or when you felt the nearness of God.

God is like _____

_____

God does _____

_____

I feel the nearness of God when _____

_____

Sometimes I think God is just like my Dad
when he holds the back seat of my new two wheel bicycle
just long enough for me to catch my balance.
Then he lets go, and I ride all by myself!
But it's nice to know he's running right alongside me.

What Is God Like?

The first stories in the Bible talk about God as creator. They tell about God making the world and everything in it. There is a song in the Bible called **Psalm 8** in which the author talks about some of the things God has made.

It's as if the person who wrote the psalm looked at many things in the world and said, "Wow! God, the world is filled with awesome things!"

Do you ever wonder, "Who is God?"

What are things in the world that make you say "Wow!"?
Write a prayer or blessing about these things.

I wonder if God has a big lap to curl up in,
just like my Mom's, and strong arms, just like Dad's
to lift me up and catch me when I fall.

I wonder if God has strong hands
to hold me tight, just like Mom's, and big shoulders,
just like Dad's, to carry me when I am tired.

What makes you feel safe and warm and loved?

Do you ever ask yourself, "What is God like?"
Lots of people do that.
People think of God in lots of different
ways: as father, mother, creator, friend.
How do you like to think of God?
What do you think God might look like?
What things make you think about God:
what colors, feelings, smells, sounds?

Can you draw a picture of God? It's difficult
Draw a picture of what God might be like o
a picture of something God does. Or, draw a
picture of a time when you felt God's presence o
when you felt the nearness of God.

God is like _____

_____

God does _____

_____

I feel the nearness of God when _____

_____

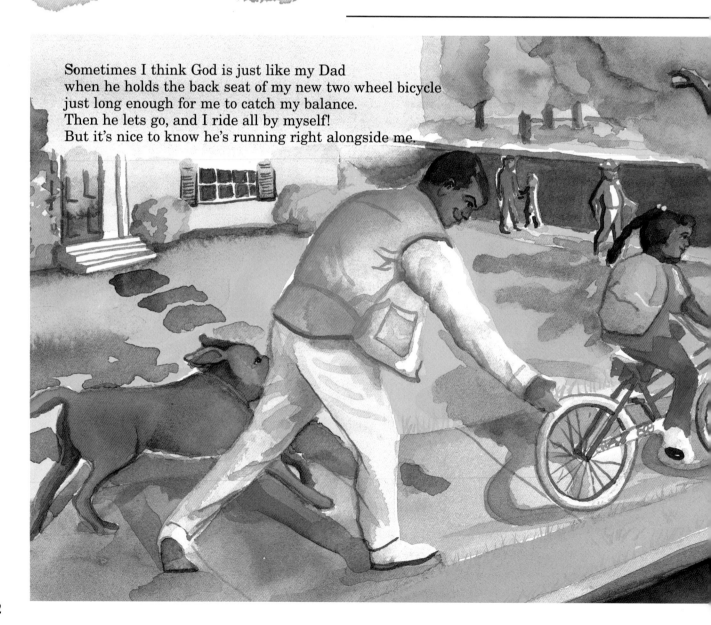

Sometimes I think God is just like my Dad
when he holds the back seat of my new two wheel bicycle
just long enough for me to catch my balance.
Then he lets go, and I ride all by myself!
But it's nice to know he's running right alongside me.

Do you ever feel afraid to try something new? Sometimes your hands get sweaty or your stomach feels like there are butterflies in it. Everyone feels that way.

At times like this someone can help you take the first step, and then you find you can do what you were afraid of and it's fun.

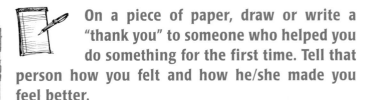

On a piece of paper, draw or write a "thank you" to someone who helped you do something for the first time. Tell that person how you felt and how he/she made you feel better.

Thank you _____

You made me feel _____

_____

_____

_____

Sometimes I think God is just like my Mom
when she helps me look both ways in crossing the street
and then lets me go—all by myself!
But it's nice to know she's still watching me at the corner.

*What makes you feel big enough to do something,
all by yourself, for the very first time?*

My Mom and I went shopping in the city. There in the middle of a crowded department store was a little boy.

He was alone and crying.

My Mom held his hands in hers and took him to a clerk who worked at the store. The clerk made an announcement over the loudspeaker saying that a little boy was lost.

Before long, his mom came and gave him a great big hug. My Mom hugged me, too. I'm not sure why.

One of the things I like about my Mom is her hands. When I was just a baby, my Mom says her hands rocked the cradle, so I wouldn't cry.

I wonder if God's hands rock the world.

How can your hands help God's hands?

God made everything in the world, but the world is not finished. People are God's partners, and we help God in creating and making the world a better place. There's a phrase in Hebrew, *tikkun olam*, which means "repairing the world." It reminds us that God invites us to help repair the hurts and the cracks in the world.

Make some helping hands: Trace your hand on a piece of paper and write on it something you could do to help someone else. Cut it out and give it to him or her. Make lots!

On one piece of paper, draw a picture of something in the world that seems unfair, or a situation where someone feels hurt. On another piece of paper, draw or write a way you could help change that. Attach this to the first picture with a bandage you use to make a sore feel better.

Do you ever feel afraid to try something new? Sometimes your hands get sweaty or your stomach feels like there are butterflies in it. Everyone feels that way.

At times like this someone can help you take the first step, and then you find you can do what you were afraid of and it's fun.

On a piece of paper, draw or write a "thank you" to someone who helped you do something for the first time. Tell that person how you felt and how he/she made you feel better.

Thank you _____

You made me feel _____

_____

_____

_____

Sometimes I think God is just like my Mom
when she helps me look both ways in crossing the street
and then lets me go—all by myself!
But it's nice to know she's still watching me at the corner.

*What makes you feel big enough to do something,
all by yourself, for the very first time?*

3

My Mom and I went shopping in the city. There in the middle of a crowded department store was a little boy.

He was alone and crying.

My Mom held his hands in hers and took him to a clerk who worked at the store. The clerk made an announcement over the loudspeaker saying that a little boy was lost.

Before long, his mom came and gave him a great big hug. My Mom hugged me, too. I'm not sure why.

One of the things I like about my Mom is her hands. When I was just a baby, my Mom says her hands rocked the cradle, so I wouldn't cry.

I wonder if God's hands rock the world.

How can your hands help God's hands?

God made everything in the world, but the world is not finished. People are God's partners, and we help God in creating and making the world a better place. There's a phrase in Hebrew, *tikkun olam,* which means "repairing the world." It reminds us that God invites us to help repair the hurts and the cracks in the world.

Make some helping hands: Trace your hand on a piece of paper and write on it something you could do to help someone else. Cut it out and give it to him or her. Make lots!

On one piece of paper, draw a picture of something in the world that seems unfair, or a situation where someone feels hurt. On another piece of paper, draw or write a way you could help change that. Attach this to the first picture with a bandage you use to make a sore feel better.

Do you ever feel afraid to try something new? Sometimes your hands get sweaty or your stomach feels like there are butterflies in it. Everyone feels that way.
At times like this someone can help you take the first step, and then you find you can do what you were afraid of and it's fun.

On a piece of paper, draw or write a "thank you" to someone who helped you do something for the first time. Tell that person how you felt and how he/she made you feel better.

Thank you _____

You made me feel _____

_____

_____

Sometimes I think God is just like my Mom
when she helps me look both ways in crossing the street
and then lets me go—all by myself!
But it's nice to know she's still watching me at the corner.

*What makes you feel big enough to do something,
all by yourself, for the very first time?*

My Mom and I went shopping in the city. There in the middle of a crowded department store was a little boy.

He was alone and crying.

My Mom held his hands in hers and took him to a clerk who worked at the store. The clerk made an announcement over the loudspeaker saying that a little boy was lost.

Before long, his mom came and gave him a great big hug. My Mom hugged me, too. I'm not sure why.

One of the things I like about my Mom is her hands. When I was just a baby, my Mom says her hands rocked the cradle, so I wouldn't cry.

I wonder if God's hands rock the world.

How can your hands help God's hands?

God made everything in the world, but the world is not finished. People are God's partners, and we help God in creating and making the world a better place. There's a phrase in Hebrew, *tikkun olam,* which means "repairing the world." It reminds us that God invites us to help repair the hurts and the cracks in the world.

Make some helping hands: Trace your hand on a piece of paper and write on it something you could do to help someone else. Cut it out and give it to him or her. Make lots!

On one piece of paper, draw a picture of something in the world that seems unfair, or a situation where someone feels hurt. On another piece of paper, draw or write a way you could help change that. Attach this to the first picture with a bandage you use to make a sore feel better.

Do you ever feel afraid to try something new?
Sometimes your hands get sweaty or your
stomach feels like there are butterflies in it.
Everyone feels that way.
At times like this someone can help you
take the first step, and then you find you can
do what you were afraid of and it's fun.

On a piece of paper, draw or write a "thank you" to someone who helped you do something for the first time. Tell that person how you felt and how he/she made you feel better.

Thank you _____

You made me feel _____

_____

_____

Sometimes I think God is just like my Mom
when she helps me look both ways in crossing the street
and then lets me go—all by myself!
But it's nice to know she's still watching me at the corner.

*What makes you feel big enough to do something,
all by yourself, for the very first time?*

My Mom and I went shopping in the city.
There in the middle of a crowded
department store was a little boy.
    He was alone and crying.
    My Mom held his hands in hers and
took him to a clerk who worked at the store.
The clerk made an announcement over the
loudspeaker saying that a little boy was lost.

Before long, his mom came and gave him a
great big hug. My Mom hugged me, too.
I'm not sure why.

One of the things I like about my Mom is her
hands. When I was just a baby, my Mom says
her hands rocked the cradle, so I wouldn't cry.
    I wonder if God's hands rock the world.

How can your hands help God's hands?

God made everything in the world, but the world is not finished. People are God's
partners, and we help God in creating and making the world a better place. There's
a phrase in Hebrew, *tikkun olam,* which means "repairing the world."
It reminds us that God invites us to help repair the hurts and the cracks
in the world.

Make some helping
hands: Trace your hand
on a piece of paper and
write on it something you could do
to help someone else. Cut it out and
give it to him or her. Make lots!

On one piece of paper, draw a picture of
something in the world that seems
unfair, or a situation where someone
feels hurt. On another piece of paper, draw or
write a way you could help change that. Attach
this to the first picture with a bandage you use to
make a sore feel better.

Do you ever feel afraid to try something new?
Sometimes your hands get sweaty or your
stomach feels like there are butterflies in it.
Everyone feels that way.
At times like this someone can help you
take the first step, and then you find you can
do what you were afraid of and it's fun.

On a piece of paper, draw or write a
"thank you" to someone who helped you
do something for the first time. Tell that
person how you felt and how he/she made you
feel better.

Thank you _____

You made me feel _____

_____

_____

Sometimes I think God is just like my Mom
when she helps me look both ways in crossing the street
and then lets me go—all by myself!
But it's nice to know she's still watching me at the corner.

*What makes you feel big enough to do something,
all by yourself, for the very first time?*

3

My Mom and I went shopping in the city. There in the middle of a crowded department store was a little boy.

He was alone and crying.

My Mom held his hands in hers and took him to a clerk who worked at the store. The clerk made an announcement over the loudspeaker saying that a little boy was lost.

Before long, his mom came and gave him a great big hug. My Mom hugged me, too. I'm not sure why.

One of the things I like about my Mom is her hands. When I was just a baby, my Mom says her hands rocked the cradle, so I wouldn't cry.

I wonder if God's hands rock the world.

How can your hands help God's hands?

God made everything in the world, but the world is not finished. People are God's partners, and we help God in creating and making the world a better place. There's a phrase in Hebrew, *tikkun olam*, which means "repairing the world." It reminds us that God invites us to help repair the hurts and the cracks in the world.

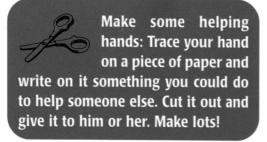

Make some helping hands: Trace your hand on a piece of paper and write on it something you could do to help someone else. Cut it out and give it to him or her. Make lots!

On one piece of paper, draw a picture of something in the world that seems unfair, or a situation where someone feels hurt. On another piece of paper, draw or write a way you could help change that. Attach this to the first picture with a bandage you use to make a sore feel better.

Do you ever feel afraid to try something new? Sometimes your hands get sweaty or your stomach feels like there are butterflies in it. Everyone feels that way.
At times like this someone can help you take the first step, and then you find you can do what you were afraid of and it's fun.

On a piece of paper, draw or write a "thank you" to someone who helped you do something for the first time. Tell that person how you felt and how he/she made you feel better.

Thank you _____

You made me feel _____

_____

_____

_____

Sometimes I think God is just like my Mom
when she helps me look both ways in crossing the street
and then lets me go—all by myself!
But it's nice to know she's still watching me at the corner.

*What makes you feel big enough to do something,
all by yourself, for the very first time?*

3

My Mom and I went shopping in the city.
There in the middle of a crowded
department store was a little boy.
　　He was alone and crying.
　　My Mom held his hands in hers and
took him to a clerk who worked at the store.
The clerk made an announcement over the
loudspeaker saying that a little boy was lost.

Before long, his mom came and gave him a
great big hug. My Mom hugged me, too.
I'm not sure why.

One of the things I like about my Mom is her
hands. When I was just a baby, my Mom says
her hands rocked the cradle, so I wouldn't cry.
　　I wonder if God's hands rock the world.

How can your hands help God's hands?

God made everything in the world, but the world is not finished. People are God's
partners, and we help God in creating and making the world a better place. There's
a phrase in Hebrew, *tikkun olam,* which means "repairing the world."
It reminds us that God invites us to help repair the hurts and the cracks
in the world.

Make some helping hands: Trace your hand on a piece of paper and write on it something you could do to help someone else. Cut it out and give it to him or her. Make lots!

On one piece of paper, draw a picture of something in the world that seems unfair, or a situation where someone feels hurt. On another piece of paper, draw or write a way you could help change that. Attach this to the first picture with a bandage you use to make a sore feel better.

Do you ever feel afraid to try something new?
Sometimes your hands get sweaty or your
stomach feels like there are butterflies in it.
Everyone feels that way.
At times like this someone can help you
take the first step, and then you find you can
do what you were afraid of and it's fun.

On a piece of paper, draw or write a
"thank you" to someone who helped you
do something for the first time. Tell that
person how you felt and how he/she made you
feel better.

Thank you _____

You made me feel _____

_____

_____

_____

Sometimes I think God is just like my Mom
when she helps me look both ways in crossing the street
and then lets me go—all by myself!
But it's nice to know she's still watching me at the corner.

*What makes you feel big enough to do something,
all by yourself, for the very first time?*

My Mom and I went shopping in the city. There in the middle of a crowded department store was a little boy.

He was alone and crying.

My Mom held his hands in hers and took him to a clerk who worked at the store. The clerk made an announcement over the loudspeaker saying that a little boy was lost.

Before long, his mom came and gave him a great big hug. My Mom hugged me, too. I'm not sure why.

One of the things I like about my Mom is her hands. When I was just a baby, my Mom says her hands rocked the cradle, so I wouldn't cry. I wonder if God's hands rock the world. •

How can your hands help God's hands?

God made everything in the world, but the world is not finished. People are God's partners, and we help God in creating and making the world a better place. There's a phrase in Hebrew, *tikkun olam,* which means "repairing the world." It reminds us that God invites us to help repair the hurts and the cracks in the world.

Make some helping hands: Trace your hand on a piece of paper and write on it something you could do to help someone else. Cut it out and give it to him or her. Make lots!

On one piece of paper, draw a picture of something in the world that seems unfair, or a situation where someone feels hurt. On another piece of paper, draw or write a way you could help change that. Attach this to the first picture with a bandage you use to make a sore feel better.

Do you ever feel afraid to try something new? Sometimes your hands get sweaty or your stomach feels like there are butterflies in it. Everyone feels that way.
At times like this someone can help you take the first step, and then you find you can do what you were afraid of and it's fun.

On a piece of paper, draw or write a "thank you" to someone who helped you do something for the first time. Tell that person how you felt and how he/she made you feel better.

Thank you _____

You made me feel _____

_____

_____

_____

Sometimes I think God is just like my Mom
when she helps me look both ways in crossing the street
and then lets me go—all by myself!
But it's nice to know she's still watching me at the corner.

*What makes you feel big enough to do something,
all by yourself, for the very first time?*

My Mom and I went shopping in the city. There in the middle of a crowded department store was a little boy.

He was alone and crying.

My Mom held his hands in hers and took him to a clerk who worked at the store. The clerk made an announcement over the loudspeaker saying that a little boy was lost.

Before long, his mom came and gave him a great big hug. My Mom hugged me, too. I'm not sure why.

One of the things I like about my Mom is her hands. When I was just a baby, my Mom says her hands rocked the cradle, so I wouldn't cry. I wonder if God's hands rock the world. ·

How can your hands help God's hands?

God made everything in the world, but the world is not finished. People are God's partners, and we help God in creating and making the world a better place. There's a phrase in Hebrew, *tikkun olam*, which means "repairing the world." It reminds us that God invites us to help repair the hurts and the cracks in the world.

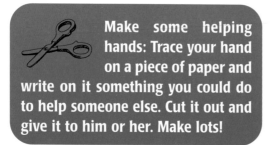

Make some helping hands: Trace your hand on a piece of paper and write on it something you could do to help someone else. Cut it out and give it to him or her. Make lots!

On one piece of paper, draw a picture of something in the world that seems unfair, or a situation where someone feels hurt. On another piece of paper, draw or write a way you could help change that. Attach this to the first picture with a bandage you use to make a sore feel better.

Deuteronomy 6:4–5 reminds us that we should love God with our whole being. Every part of us should show others we love God. Our hands can help others. Our feet can dance in celebration. Our mouths can sing songs of praise, or speak out for justice and fairness. Everything we do should show others that we love God. That's what it means to be God's paintbrush! In the Bible, and throughout history, people have often danced in response to God's love. Dancing is one way we can use our whole body to say, "Thank you, God" or "Praise God."

When I help a friend,
when I make someone smile,
I think I am part of God's dance.

Can you dance God's dance?

What would it look like?

Put on some music and move your body to it. Imagine you are talking to God with your body. What are you saying?

1

We are all unique. We are all different. God wants each of us to be a special paintbrush. Even our fingerprints are all different! Press your fingers on a stamp pad, then press them carefully here:

(BE SURE TO WASH YOUR FINGERS afterwards—ink will stain if you're not careful.) Now, invite friends or family members to do this, and look at the fingerprints under a magnifying glass—each one is different! With a marker, draw arms and legs and a face on your fingerprint, to make a unique little person.

My friend is great at math.
She always gets 100 on her tests.
My brother is captain of his baseball team.
He always gets home runs.

Sometimes when I get lots of red X's
all over my math paper,
I think I'd like to be just like my friend.

When I get up to bat and strike out,
I think I'd like to be just like my brother.

Play charades with your friends, acting out things you can do or talents that you have.

Deuteronomy 6:4–5 reminds us that we should love God with our whole being. Every part of us should show others we love God. Our hands can help others. Our feet can dance in celebration. Our mouths can sing songs of praise, or speak out for justice and fairness. Everything we do should show others that we love God. That's what it means to be God's paintbrush! In the Bible, and throughout history, people have often danced in response to God's love. Dancing is one way we can use our whole body to say, "Thank you, God" or "Praise God."

When I help a friend,
when I make someone smile,
I think I am part of God's dance.

Can you dance God's dance?

What would it look like?

Put on some music and move your body to it. Imagine you are talking to God with your body. What are you saying?

We are all unique. We are all different. God wants each of us to be a special paintbrush. Even our fingerprints are all different! Press your fingers on a stamp pad, then press them carefully here:

(BE SURE TO WASH YOUR FINGERS afterwards—ink will stain if you're not careful.) Now, invite friends or family members to do this, and look at the fingerprints under a magnifying glass—each one is different! With a marker, draw arms and legs and a face on your fingerprint, to make a unique little person.

My friend is great at math.
She always gets 100 on her tests.
My brother is captain of his baseball team.
He always gets home runs.

Sometimes when I get lots of red X's
all over my math paper,
I think I'd like to be just like my friend.

When I get up to bat and strike out,
I think I'd like to be just like my brother.

Play charades with your friends, acting out things you can do or talents that you have.

Deuteronomy 6:4–5 reminds us that we should love God with our whole being. Every part of us should show others we love God. Our hands can help others. Our feet can dance in celebration. Our mouths can sing songs of praise, or speak out for justice and fairness. Everything we do should show others that we love God. That's what it means to be God's paintbrush! In the Bible, and throughout history, people have often danced in response to God's love. Dancing is one way we can use our whole body to say, "Thank you, God" or "Praise God."

When I help a friend,
when I make someone smile,
I think I am part of God's dance.

Can you dance God's dance?

What would it look like?

Put on some music and move your body to it. Imagine you are talking to God with your body. What are you saying?

We are all unique. We are all different. God wants each of us to be a special paintbrush. Even our fingerprints are all different! Press your fingers on a stamp pad, then press them carefully here:

(BE SURE TO WASH YOUR FINGERS afterwards—ink will stain if you're not careful.) Now, invite friends or family members to do this, and look at the fingerprints under a magnifying glass—each one is different! With a marker, draw arms and legs and a face on your fingerprint, to make a unique little person.

My friend is great at math.
She always gets 100 on her tests.
My brother is captain of his baseball team.
He always gets home runs.

Sometimes when I get lots of red X's
all over my math paper,
I think I'd like to be just like my friend.

When I get up to bat and strike out,
I think I'd like to be just like my brother.

Play charades with your friends, acting out things you can do or talents that you have.

Deuteronomy 6:4–5 reminds us that we should love God with our whole being. Every part of us should show others we love God. Our hands can help others. Our feet can dance in celebration. Our mouths can sing songs of praise, or speak out for justice and fairness. Everything we do should show others that we love God. That's what it means to be God's paintbrush! In the Bible, and throughout history, people have often danced in response to God's love. Dancing is one way we can use our whole body to say, "Thank you, God" or "Praise God."

When I help a friend,
when I make someone smile,
I think I am part of God's dance.

Can you dance God's dance?

What would it look like?

Put on some music and move your body to it. Imagine you are talking to God with your body. What are you saying?

1

We are all unique. We are all different. God wants each of us to be a special paintbrush. Even our fingerprints are all different! Press your fingers on a stamp pad, then press them carefully here:

(BE SURE TO WASH YOUR FINGERS afterwards—ink will stain if you're not careful.) Now, invite friends or family members to do this, and look at the fingerprints under a magnifying glass—each one is different! With a marker, draw arms and legs and a face on your fingerprint, to make a unique little person.

My friend is great at math.
She always gets 100 on her tests.
My brother is captain of his baseball team.
He always gets home runs.

Sometimes when I get lots of red X's
all over my math paper,
I think I'd like to be just like my friend.

When I get up to bat and strike out,
I think I'd like to be just like my brother.

Play charades with your friends, acting out things you can do or talents that you have.

Deuteronomy 6:4–5 reminds us that we should love God with our whole being. Every part of us should show others we love God. Our hands can help others. Our feet can dance in celebration. Our mouths can sing songs of praise, or speak out for justice and fairness. Everything we do should show others that we love God. That's what it means to be God's paintbrush! In the Bible, and throughout history, people have often danced in response to God's love. Dancing is one way we can use our whole body to say, "Thank you, God" or "Praise God."

When I help a friend,
when I make someone smile,
I think I am part of God's dance.

Can you dance God's dance?

What would it look like?

Put on some music and move your body to it. Imagine you are talking to God with your body. What are you saying?

We are all unique. We are all different. God wants each of us to be a special paintbrush. Even our fingerprints are all different! Press your fingers on a stamp pad, then press them carefully here:

(BE SURE TO WASH YOUR FINGERS afterwards—ink will stain if you're not careful.) Now, invite friends or family members to do this, and look at the fingerprints under a magnifying glass—each one is different! With a marker, draw arms and legs and a face on your fingerprint, to make a unique little person.

My friend is great at math.
She always gets 100 on her tests.
My brother is captain of his baseball team.
He always gets home runs.

Sometimes when I get lots of red X's
all over my math paper,
I think I'd like to be just like my friend.

When I get up to bat and strike out,
I think I'd like to be just like my brother.

Play charades with your friends, acting out things you can do or talents that you have.

Deuteronomy 6:4–5 reminds us that we should love God with our whole being. Every part of us should show others we love God. Our hands can help others. Our feet can dance in celebration. Our mouths can sing songs of praise, or speak out for justice and fairness. Everything we do should show others that we love God. That's what it means to be God's paintbrush! In the Bible, and throughout history, people have often danced in response to God's love. Dancing is one way we can use our whole body to say, "Thank you, God" or "Praise God."

When I help a friend,
when I make someone smile,
I think I am part of God's dance.

Can you dance God's dance?

What would it look like?

Put on some music and move your body to it. Imagine you are talking to God with your body. What are you saying?

We are all unique. We are all different. God wants each of us to be a special paintbrush. Even our fingerprint are all different! Press your fingers on a stamp pad, then press them carefully here:

(BE SURE TO WASH YOUR FINGERS afterwards—ink will stain if you're not careful.) Now, invite friends or family members to do this, and look at the fingerprints under a magnifying glass—each one is different! With a marker, draw arms and legs and a face on your fingerprint, to make a unique little person.

My friend is great at math.
She always gets 100 on her tests.
My brother is captain of his baseball team.
He always gets home runs.

Sometimes when I get lots of red X's
all over my math paper,
I think I'd like to be just like my friend.

When I get up to bat and strike out,
I think I'd like to be just like my brother.

Play charades with your friends, acting out things you can do or talents that you have.

Deuteronomy 6:4–5 reminds us that we should love God with our whole being. Every part of us should show others we love God. Our hands can help others. Our feet can dance in celebration. Our mouths can sing songs of praise, or speak out for justice and fairness. Everything we do should show others that we love God. That's what it means to be God's paintbrush! In the Bible, and throughout history, people have often danced in response to God's love. Dancing is one way we can use our whole body to say, "Thank you, God" or "Praise God."

When I help a friend,
when I make someone smile,
I think I am part of God's dance.

Can you dance God's dance?

What would it look like?

Put on some music and move your body to it. Imagine you are talking to God with your body. What are you saying?

We are all unique. We are all different. God wants each of us to be a special paintbrush. Even our fingerprints are all different! Press your fingers on a stamp pad, then press them carefully here:

(BE SURE TO WASH YOUR FINGERS afterwards—ink will stain if you're not careful.) Now, invite friends or family members to do this, and look at the fingerprints under a magnifying glass—each one is different! With a marker, draw arms and legs and a face on your fingerprint, to make a unique little person.

My friend is great at math.
She always gets 100 on her tests.
My brother is captain of his baseball team.
He always gets home runs.

Sometimes when I get lots of red X's
all over my math paper,
I think I'd like to be just like my friend.

When I get up to bat and strike out,
I think I'd like to be just like my brother.

Play charades with your friends, acting out things you can do or talents that you have.

2

Deuteronomy 6:4–5 reminds us that we should love God with our whole being. Every part of us should show others we love God. Our hands can help others. Our feet can dance in celebration. Our mouths can sing songs of praise, or speak out for justice and fairness. Everything we do should show others that we love God. That's what it means to be God's paintbrush! In the Bible, and throughout history, people have often danced in response to God's love. Dancing is one way we can use our whole body to say, "Thank you, God" or "Praise God."

When I help a friend,
when I make someone smile,
I think I am part of God's dance.

Can you dance God's dance?

What would it look like?

Put on some music and move your body to it. Imagine you are talking to God with your body. What are you saying?

We are all unique. We are all different. God wants each of us to be a special paintbrush. Even our fingerprints are all different! Press your fingers on a stamp pad, then press them carefully here:

(BE SURE TO WASH YOUR FINGERS afterwards—ink will stain if you're not careful.) Now, invite friends or family members to do this, and look at the fingerprints under a magnifying glass—each one is different! With a marker, draw arms and legs and a face on your fingerprint, to make a unique little person.

My friend is great at math.
She always gets 100 on her tests.
My brother is captain of his baseball team.
He always gets home runs.

Sometimes when I get lots of red X's
all over my math paper,
I think I'd like to be just like my friend.

When I get up to bat and strike out,
I think I'd like to be just like my brother.

Play charades with your friends, acting out things you can do or talents that you have.

Create some "my gifts" cards: on pieces of paper, write "My gift to my sister (or brother, Mom, Dad, neighbor, etc.) is. . ." Fill this in with things you can share with them. Remember, the best things you can share are those that make you special, like a smile, help with a household chore, a trip to the park, enjoying a special moment together, etc.

But then I think,
    I enjoy gymnastics.
    I can do one-handed
    cartwheels!
    I am glad to be me!

Perhaps God gave each of us
a special gift that makes us
different from anyone else,
and when we share that gift —
    God is happy.

What is your gift?

How do you share your gift?

What do you like about yourself? Make a list of at least 3 things:

_____   _____   _____

What do you like about your best friend? Make a list of at least 3 things:

_____   _____   _____

Tell other people the things you like about them.

Often we say that the things we do "color" our lives.
What color is your life?
What color is happiness? sadness? forgiveness? loneliness?
How can we color the world?

Sometimes on a bright day
when I close my eyes real tight,
I see all kinds of colors —
green and purple and red and blue.
I think these are just like God's colors.

I know God's colors are in me, too.
And I can paint with God's paintbrush.

Planting a garden, fixing up a play-ground, picking up litter, recycling, visiting the sick, respecting one another—these are all ways we can help our world be a better place. And they are all good projects we can do with others. Get together with some friends, or your family, and make some plans to do something special that can help color the world.

Create some "my gifts" cards: on pieces of paper, write "My gift to my sister (or brother, Mom, Dad, neighbor, etc.) is..." Fill this in with things you can share with them. Remember, the best things you can share are those that make you special, like a smile, help with a household chore, a trip to the park, enjoying a special moment together, etc.

But then I think,
I enjoy gymnastics.
I can do one-handed cartwheels!
I am glad to be me!

Perhaps God gave each of us a special gift that makes us different from anyone else, and when we share that gift — God is happy.

What is your gift?

How do you share your gift?

What do you like about yourself? Make a list of at least 3 things:

_____   _____   _____

What do you like about your best friend? Make a list of at least 3 things:

_____   _____   _____

Tell other people the things you like about them.

3

Often we say that the things we do "color" our lives.
What color is your life?
What color is happiness? sadness? forgiveness? loneliness?
How can we color the world?

Sometimes on a bright day
when I close my eyes real tight,
I see all kinds of colors —
green and purple and red and blue.
I think these are just like God's colors.

I know God's colors are in me, too.
And I can paint with God's paintbrush.

 Planting a garden, fixing up a playground, picking up litter, recycling, visiting the sick, respecting one another—these are all ways we can help our world be a better place. And they are all good projects we can do with others. Get together with some friends, or your family, and make some plans to do something special that can help color the world.

Create some "my gifts" cards: on pieces of paper, write "My gift to my sister (or brother, Mom, Dad, neighbor, etc.) is..." Fill this in with things you can share with them. Remember, the best things you can share are those that make you special, like a smile, help with a household chore, a trip to the park, enjoying a special moment together, etc.

But then I think,
   I enjoy gymnastics.
   I can do one-handed
   cartwheels!
   I am glad to be me!

Perhaps God gave each of us
a special gift that makes us
different from anyone else,
and when we share that gift —
   God is happy.

What is your gift?

How do you share your gift?

What do you like about yourself? Make a list of at least 3 things:

_____ _____ _____

What do you like about your best friend? Make a list of at least 3 things:

_____ _____ _____

Tell other people the things you like about them.

Often we say that the things we do "color" our lives.
What color is your life?
What color is happiness? sadness? forgiveness? loneliness?
How can we color the world?

Sometimes on a bright day
when I close my eyes real tight,
I see all kinds of colors —
green and purple and red and blue.
I think these are just like God's colors.

I know God's colors are in me, too.
And I can paint with God's paintbrush.

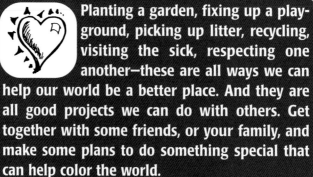

Planting a garden, fixing up a playground, picking up litter, recycling, visiting the sick, respecting one another—these are all ways we can help our world be a better place. And they are all good projects we can do with others. Get together with some friends, or your family, and make some plans to do something special that can help color the world.

Create some "my gifts" cards: on pieces of paper, write "My gift to my sister (or brother, Mom, Dad, neighbor, etc.) is. . ." Fill this in with things you can share with them. Remember, the best things you can share are those that make you special, like a smile, help with a household chore, a trip to the park, enjoying a special moment together, etc.

But then I think,
    I enjoy gymnastics.
    I can do one-handed
    cartwheels!
    I am glad to be me!

Perhaps God gave each of us
a special gift that makes us
different from anyone else,
and when we share that gift —
    God is happy.

What is your gift?

How do you share your gift?

hat do you like about yourself? Make a list of at least 3 things:

_____   _____   _____

hat do you like about your best friend? Make a list of at least 3 things:

_____   _____   _____

l other people the things you like about them.

3

Often we say that the things we do "color" our lives.
What color is your life?
What color is happiness? sadness? forgiveness? loneliness?
How can we color the world?

Sometimes on a bright day
when I close my eyes real tight,
I see all kinds of colors —
green and purple and red and blue.
I think these are just like God's colors.

I know God's colors are in me, too.
And I can paint with God's paintbrush.

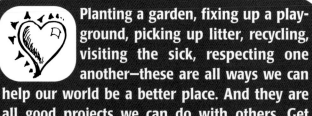

Planting a garden, fixing up a playground, picking up litter, recycling, visiting the sick, respecting one another—these are all ways we can help our world be a better place. And they are all good projects we can do with others. Get together with some friends, or your family, and make some plans to do something special that can help color the world.

But then I think,
I enjoy gymnastics.
I can do one-handed cartwheels!
I am glad to be me!

Perhaps God gave each of us a special gift that makes us different from anyone else, and when we share that gift — God is happy.

What is your gift?

How do you share your gift?

hat do you like about yourself? Make a list of at least 3 things:

_____   _____   _____

hat do you like about your best friend? Make a list of at least 3 things:

_____   _____   _____

ll other people the things you like about them.

Often we say that the things we do "color" our lives.
What color is your life?
What color is happiness? sadness? forgiveness? loneliness?
How can we color the world?

Sometimes on a bright day
when I close my eyes real tight,
I see all kinds of colors —
green and purple and red and blue.
I think these are just like God's colors.

I know God's colors are in me, too.
And I can paint with God's paintbrush.

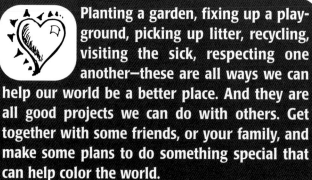

Planting a garden, fixing up a playground, picking up litter, recycling, visiting the sick, respecting one another—these are all ways we can help our world be a better place. And they are all good projects we can do with others. Get together with some friends, or your family, and make some plans to do something special that can help color the world.

Create some "my gifts" cards: on pieces of paper, write "My gift to my sister (or brother, Mom, Dad, neighbor, etc.) is. . ." Fill this in with things you can share with them. Remember, the best things you can share are those that make you special, like a smile, help with a household chore, a trip to the park, enjoying a special moment together, etc.

But then I think,
     I enjoy gymnastics.
     I can do one-handed
     cartwheels!
     I am glad to be me!

Perhaps God gave each of us a special gift that makes us different from anyone else, and when we share that gift — God is happy.

What is your gift?

How do you share your gift?

What do you like about yourself? Make a list of at least 3 things:

_____   _____   _____

What do you like about your best friend? Make a list of at least 3 things:

_____   _____   _____

Tell other people the things you like about them.

3

Often we say that the things we do "color" our lives.
What color is your life?
What color is happiness? sadness? forgiveness? loneliness?
How can we color the world?

Sometimes on a bright day
when I close my eyes real tight,
I see all kinds of colors —
green and purple and red and blue.
I think these are just like God's colors.

I know God's colors are in me, too.
And I can paint with God's paintbrush.

Planting a garden, fixing up a play-ground, picking up litter, recycling, visiting the sick, respecting one another—these are all ways we can help our world be a better place. And they are all good projects we can do with others. Get together with some friends, or your family, and make some plans to do something special that can help color the world.

But then I think,
I enjoy gymnastics.
I can do one-handed cartwheels!
I am glad to be me!

Perhaps God gave each of us a special gift that makes us different from anyone else, and when we share that gift — God is happy.

What is your gift?

How do you share your gift?

at do you like about yourself? Make a list of at least 3 things:

_____   _____   _____

at do you like about your best friend? Make a list of at least 3 things:

_____   _____   _____

other people the things you like about them.

3

Often we say that the things we do "color" our lives.
What color is your life?
What color is happiness? sadness? forgiveness? loneliness?
How can we color the world?

Sometimes on a bright day
when I close my eyes real tight,
I see all kinds of colors —
green and purple and red and blue.
I think these are just like God's colors.

I know God's colors are in me, too.
And I can paint with God's paintbrush.

Planting a garden, fixing up a playground, picking up litter, recycling,
visiting the sick, respecting one
another—these are all ways we can
help our world be a better place. And they are
all good projects we can do with others. Get
together with some friends, or your family, and
make some plans to do something special that
can help color the world.

Create some "my gifts" cards: on pieces of paper, write "My gift to my sister (or brother, Mom, Dad, neighbor, etc.) is..." Fill this in with things you can share with them. Remember, the best things you can share are those that make you special, like a smile, help with a household chore, a trip to the park, enjoying a special moment together, etc.

But then I think,
I enjoy gymnastics.
I can do one-handed
cartwheels!
I am glad to be me!

Perhaps God gave each of us a special gift that makes us different from anyone else, and when we share that gift — God is happy.

What is your gift?

How do you share your gift?

What do you like about yourself? Make a list of at least 3 things:

_____   _____   _____

What do you like about your best friend? Make a list of at least 3 things:

_____   _____   _____

Tell other people the things you like about them.

Often we say that the things we do "color" our lives.
What color is your life?
What color is happiness? sadness? forgiveness? loneliness?
How can we color the world?

Sometimes on a bright day
when I close my eyes real tight,
I see all kinds of colors —
green and purple and red and blue.
I think these are just like God's colors.

I know God's colors are in me, too.
And I can paint with God's paintbrush.

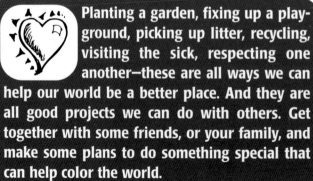

Planting a garden, fixing up a playground, picking up litter, recycling, visiting the sick, respecting one another—these are all ways we can help our world be a better place. And they are all good projects we can do with others. Get together with some friends, or your family, and make some plans to do something special that can help color the world.